Spotlight on
ANCIENT CIVILIZATIONS
ROME

Ancient Roman DAILY LIFE

Amelie von Zumbusch

Published in 2014 by The Rosen Publishing Group, Inc.
29 East 21st Street, New York, NY 10010

First Edition

Book Design: Kate Vlachos
Layout Design: Andrew Povolny

Photo Credits: Cover David Sutherland/Photographer's Choice/Getty Images; pp. 4, 5, 7, 8, 9, 10, 11, 13, 18, 22 DEA/A. Dagli Orti/De Agostini Picture Library/ Getty Images; pp. 12, 17 Leemage/Universal Images Group/Getty Images; p. 14 Digitaler Lumpensammler/Flickr/Getty Images; p. 15 Russell Mountford/Lonely Planey Images/Getty Images; p. 16 Bridgeman Art Library/Getty Images; p. 19 (bottom) Martin Moos/Lonely Planet Images/Getty Images; p. 19 (top) Guenter Fischer/Getty Images; p. 21 Superstock/Getty Images.

Library of Congress Cataloging-in-Publication Data

Zumbusch, Amelie von.
Ancient Roman daily life / by Amelie von Zumbusch. — First edition.
pages cm. — (Spotlight on ancient civilizations. Rome)
Includes index.
ISBN 978-1-4777-0778-4 (library binding) — ISBN 978-1-4777-0889-7 (pbk.) —
ISBN 978-1-4777-0890-3 (6-pack)
1. Rome—Social life and customs—Juvenile literature. I. Title.
DG78.Z96 2014
937'.63—dc23

2013003198

Manufactured in the United States of America

CPSIA Compliance Information: Batch #S13PK2: For Further Information contact Rosen Publishing, New York, New York at 1-800-237-9932

CONTENTS

Roman Families	4
Getting Married in Ancient Rome	6
Roman Women	8
Kids in Ancient Rome	10
Slaves	12
Roman Homes	14
What Did the Romans Eat?	16
Fun and Games	18
Tunics and More	20
Strong Communities	22
Glossary	23
Index	24
Websites	24

Roman Families

Families were central to ancient Roman **civilization.** The head of a Roman family was the *paterfamilias*, which means "father of the household" in Latin. He was the family's oldest man. He had total power over his *familia*. This included both family members and **slaves.**

The Romans spoke a language called Latin. *Pater* means "father" in Latin. *Mater* is Latin for "mother." "Son" is *filius*, while "daughter" is *filia*.

Young boys like the one in this carving had to obey their paterfamilias. A paterfamilias' grown sons and grandsons had to obey him, too.

Newborn babies were presented to the paterfamilias, who picked them up as a sign that the family accepted the child. Children who were not picked up were **abandoned**. However, most Romans welcomed children. Continuing the family line was seen as important. A paterfamilias with no children of his own would often adopt one, especially a relative.

Getting Married in Ancient Rome

Ancient Roman marriages were often arranged. A bride's family supplied a **dowry** that might include goods, slaves, or land. In Rome's early days, marriage meant that a woman passed from her father's control to her husband's.

Later, marriages that kept women under their fathers' power became standard. These marriages let women own **property** and gave them more freedom. Divorce became more common, too. People sometimes divorced so they could remarry to join a powerful family or have children.

Weddings generally happened at the bride's family home. They included a simple ceremony, a feast, and a **procession** to the groom's house. Brides wore flame-colored veils.

In most Roman wedding ceremonies, the bride and groom held hands in front of witnesses. This was a sign that both of them agreed to be married.

Roman Women

The Romans thought that a woman's most important role was as a wife and mother. Roman **matrons**, or married women, brought up children and ran households. Wealthy women had slaves to help them. Poorer women had to do everything, including making clothing for their families, by themselves.

This painting shows a dead man's wife and children taking part in his funeral procession. Roman widows usually remarried fairly soon after their husbands died.

Women had few political rights. They could not hold office or take part in politics. Unlike in some parts of the ancient world, though, they did go out in public. In later years, they could own property and run businesses. Under Augustus and later emperors, women who had three or more children were given more freedom.

This statue of the Roman empress Messalina shows her holding her son Britannicus. Bearing children was considered a key part of a wife's role.

Kids in Ancient Rome

Like all kids, Roman children liked to play. They had toys such as dolls, balls, tops, board games, and wagons. Games like hide-and-seek were popular, too. Many kids had pet dogs. Some had pet birds, mice, or monkeys!

Some kids went to school. Tutors taught rich children at home. Students learned to read, write, and do math. They wrote with styluses on soft wax tablets. Older boys learned Greek and Latin literature and how to be great speakers.

This statue is of the emperor Nero as a child. The necklace-like thing he is wearing is a *bulla*. It was thought to protect Roman boys. They wore them until they officially became men.

Most Roman children spent a fair amount of time with their parents. However, rich children also had slaves to care for them and teach them.

Mothers taught their daughters how to run a household. Fathers taught their sons whatever they did for a living, whether it was farming, trade, or politics.

Slaves

There were many slaves in ancient Rome. Some worked long, hard hours in mines or on farms. Others worked as servants in the homes of rich Romans. Slaves also made and sold goods in shops that their masters owned. Educated slaves worked as doctors, teachers, or accountants.

This mosaic, or picture made from small pieces of tile or stone, shows a servant carrying food for a feast. Roman servants were most often slaves.

Roman slaves could be sold at any time. Owners could also rent out their slaves. This meant that the slaves worked for people other than their owners.

Many slaves were people from lands that the Romans **conquered**. Children whose parents were slaves became slaves, too. Poor Romans who were deep in debt sometimes even sold themselves or their children into slavery.

Some slaves saved enough money to buy their freedom. Masters sometimes freed slaves. Freed slaves were called freedmen and freedwomen.

Roman Homes

Most people in Roman cities lived in blocks of apartment buildings, called *insulae*. They had shops on the ground floor and a courtyard in the center. They had no heat or running water. Poor people often lived in buildings without kitchens.

These are the ruins of houses in Pompeii. Pompeii was a Roman town in Italy. It was buried in ash when a nearby volcano erupted.

This is one of the rooms in the House of the Skeleton, in Herculaneum. This Roman town was near Pompeii and was buried in the same eruption.

Rich Romans lived in a house called a *domus*. You entered it through a passageway that led to the *atrium*. This room had an opening in the roof with a pool under it. Guests were received there. An open courtyard called a *peristylium* usually lay beyond. The *tablinum,* where the paterfamilias had his office, connected the two. Smaller rooms surrounded the peristylium and atrium. Homes often had several *triclinia,* or dining rooms.

What Did the Romans Eat?

The Romans ate a small, early breakfast. Their main meal was the *cena*. Early on, it was eaten at midday. Later, it was eaten in the evening. People ate another light meal at noon or night, depending on what time their cena was.

This carving shows grapes being pressed to make wine. The Romans sometimes mixed their wine with fruits, herbs, and spices.

This mosaic shows a group of Romans enjoying an outdoor meal after a hunting trip.

The main foods for poor Romans were bread and **porridge** made of wheat. When they could afford it, they added vegetables, fish, or meat. Olive oil was used for cooking and eating. Wine was common and almost always mixed with water. Rich Romans held feasts with many courses for their friends. They often served **exotic** foods, such as peacock brains!

Fun and Games

In their free time, the Romans liked to watch thrilling and dangerous **spectacles**. There were chariot races, in which drivers in two-wheeled chariots steered teams of horses around a long track. Romans watched trained fighters called gladiators fight against each other, often to the death. People also went to theaters to watch funny plays and see people act out famous battles.

The Romans also liked listening to music. Many of the instruments Roman musicians used had originally come from Greece.

Here you can see the remains of the baths at Leptis Magna. This was a Roman city in what is now Libya.

The Romans went to public baths to relax. There, they would exercise, chat with friends, and, of course, take baths. Most public baths had different rooms with cold, warm, and hot water. Some baths also had entertainment, such as jugglers or people reciting poetry.

Gladiatorial games took place in big arenas called amphitheaters. Gladiators were classed into groups depending on the weapons they fought with.

Tunics and More

Practically everyone in Roman times wore tunics. Women's tunics reached their feet, while men's were knee-length. Slaves generally wore only a tunic, though they might wear a cloak over it on cold days. Matrons wore a dress called a *stola* over their tunics. They often wore a shawl called a *palla* over that.

Men wore tunics when they were at home or working. For formal occasions, men draped a long toga over their tunics. Only **citizens** could wear togas. Most togas were made of plain white wool. Children and certain officials wore the *toga praetexta*, which had a reddish-purple stripe.

Wealthy Roman women had complicated hairstyles and wore finely made jewelry. They wore clothing made of costly fabrics, such as silk brought from China.

Strong Communities

One of the qualities that the Romans most valued was *pietas*. Part of pietas was being devoted to one's family. It also meant being loyal to one's country and having proper respect for the gods.

The Romans saw these things as connected. A paterfamilias carried out ceremonies honoring his **ancestors** and family gods in the name of his whole family. The government was expected to look out for its citizens, like a paterfamilias cared for his family. The family was the model for the larger community.

Roman parents, like the mother watching her children play in this carving, tried to bring their children up to be good citizens.

GLOSSARY

abandoned (uh-BAN-dund) Left or given up.

ancestors (AN-ses-terz) Relatives who lived long ago.

citizens (SIH-tih-zenz) People who were live in a country or other community and have certain rights.

civilization (sih-vih-lih-ZAY-shun) People living in a certain way.

conquered (KON-kerd) Overcame.

dowry (DOW-ree) The money or property that a woman brings to her husband when they get married.

exotic (ek-ZAH-tik) Strange or unusual.

matrons (MAY-trunz) Respected married women.

porridge (POR-ij) Grain boiled with water until thick and soft, like oatmeal.

procession (pruh-SESH-un) A group of people moving along in an orderly way for a special purpose or occasion.

property (PRO-per-tee) Things a person owns.

slaves (SLAYVZ) People who are "owned" by other people and forced to work for them.

spectacles (SPEK-tuh-kulz) Striking displays or events.

INDEX

B
baths, 19
buildings, 14
businesses, 9

C
cena, 16
chariots, 18
citizens, 20, 22
civilization, 4

D
debt, 13
dowry, 6

E
emperors, 9
entertainment, 19

F
feast(s), 6, 17
foods, 17
freedom, 6, 9, 13

G
gladiators, 18
gods, 22
goods, 6, 12
government, 22

L
Latin, 4, 10

M
masters, 12–13
matrons, 8, 20
mother(s), 8, 11

P
paterfamilias, 4–5, 15, 22
politics, 9, 11
power, 4, 6
property, 6, 9

S
shops, 12, 14
slaves, 4, 6, 8, 12–13, 20

T
toga(s), 20
tunic(s), 20

W
water, 14, 17, 19

WEBSITES

Due to the changing nature of Internet links, PowerKids Press has developed an online list of websites related to the subject of this book. This site is updated regularly. Please use this link to access the list:
www.powerkidslinks.com/sacr/life/